Original title:
Shadows of Sass

Copyright © 2025 Creative Arts Management OÜ
All rights reserved.

Author: Fiona Harrington
ISBN HARDBACK: 978-1-80567-294-4
ISBN PAPERBACK: 978-1-80567-593-8

Sketches of the Sassy

In a world where quips collide,
With a wink and an easy stride,
They strut about in vibrant hue,
Leaving giggles in their queue.

With sass that sparkles like the sun,
They make the mundane feel like fun,
A flip of hair, a playful glance,
Turning boredom into a dance.

They juggle jests, oh what a sight,
With puns that tickle, pure delight,
A sassy grin, the joke's on you,
As laughter spreads like morning dew.

In every quirk and playful tease,
They weave a magic, if you please,
With every giggle, life's a blast,
In sketches bright, they ever last.

Shades of Sarcasm

In a world of winks and smirks,
Where laughter meets its match,
With every quip, a barb it lurks,
Oh, who will take the batch?

With side glances and clever quips,
They juggle words like balls of fire,
Spitting sass like candy chips,
Who knew humor could inspire?

Threads of Boldness

Dressed in neon, they strut and sway,
Fabric clashing, colors collide,
With every step, they steal the day,
Confidence worn like a wild ride.

With laughter trailing their fashion flair,
They twist the mundane into delight,
Every stitch a daring affair,
In this fabric, they shine so bright.

Essence of Edge

Witty bone and sharp-tongued grace,
They prance on the line so thin,
With jokes of pride, they hold their space,
Where laughter ends, their joy begins.

Like a jester dressed in chic attire,
They canvas life in bold, bright hue,
With every jest, they spark the fire,
Brewing fun in their daring brew.

Footsteps of Ferocity

Marching forth with cheeky style,
They tiptoe on the edge of glee,
Every stomp a playful smile,
With sass that dances wild and free.

In a world where seriousness lurks,
They dash through clouds of dreary frowns,
Unruly joy, how their heart works,
Wearing laughter like a crown.

The Pulse of Play

In the park, a laugh doth soar,
Chasing joy, we crave for more.
Bubbles burst, a silly dance,
Who knew fun could take a chance?

In hopscotch, we take a dive,
Age is naught, we feel alive.
Twists and turns, a playful chase,
Laughter's light, it sets the pace.

Hushed Haughtiness

With a wink, she struts on by,
Holding secrets, oh, so spry.
A pouty lip, a teasing glance,
Who knew pride could lead to prance?

Underneath that towering crown,
Her smirk could flip the whole town.
She twirls in shoes, just too absurd,
Yet somehow, she's never heard.

Notes of Naughtiness

Whispers dance on velvet air,
Mischief brightens every stare.
In the corner, giggles spread,
Echoes of what's left unsaid.

Chocolate stains on fingers wide,
Sneaky grins we cannot hide.
Under tables, secrets pass,
Crafty tales, we raise a glass.

Grit Beneath Grace

With elegance, they steal the show,
Yet, underfoot, they trip and glow.
A graceful bow, a clumsy fall,
Together, they just hold it all.

With poise, they dance, yet laugh out loud,
Playing tricks, they stand so proud.
Who knew charm could weave such fun,
In the light of a setting sun?

The Twinkle of Tact

In a world where whispers gleam,
Words are dressed in fancy scheme.
With a grin and glinting eyes,
Every jest becomes a prize.

Witty darts fly through the air,
You can't help but stop and stare.
Like a cat that walks on glass,
Each footfall brings a cheeky sass.

Jokes are ruffled, laughter swells,
In this dance, each story tells.
Tact is born from spark and flair,
With a twist, we play somewhere.

Watch them dodge, with glee, we trod,
As the punchlines form a façade.
With a wink, a teased remark,
Ignites the night, ignites the spark.

The Beat of Boldness

Strut your stuff on life's great stage,
Dare to turn another page.
When you tickle fate's fine nose,
Boldness thrives, and laughter grows.

Rhythm to the night we sway,
Each step a cheeky cabaret.
With pep and pizazz, we dive,
In this farce, we feel alive.

Every chuckle plays the drum,
Sounding out as we succumb.
Kick at clouds, and dance so free,
Living bold with jokes and glee.

Life's too short for dull routines,
So we flaunt our quirkiest scenes.
With a hop, a skip, and grin,
Join the fun, let's all jump in.

Remarks in the Murk

In the corners where secrets hide,
Lurks a wisecrack, full of pride.
With a laugh, we peel the dark,
As clever quips ignite a spark.

Murmurs scatter like quicksand,
With zingers sharp, we take our stand.
From shadows, laughter starts to bloom,
Transforming silence into room.

Each chuckle breaks the stagnant night,
With jokes that twinkle, pure delight.
In the murk, we dance and weave,
Fun in the corners, we believe.

As hilarity finds its way,
We spin confusion into play.
With grins and quips, we stir the pot,
In the dark, we find our plot.

Flare Beneath the Surface

Underneath the calm facade,
Lurks a flare that's bold and mad.
With wit like fireworks afloat,
We concoct a lighthearted quote.

Beneath the waves of normalcy,
A riot dances, wild and free.
In each quirk, there's life to savor,
Crafting joy with clever flavor.

Sparks will fly when laughter breaks,
And in the midst, a wisecrack wakes.
So let the bubble burst and pop,
As we unleash, we'll never stop.

Cast away the muted tones,
For vibrant jokes in playful zones.
With each jest a playful tease,
We ignite the world, and with ease.

Prowess in the Gloom

In the corners where giggles creep,
Sneaky grins far too bold to keep.
With every step, mischief does bloom,
Prowess shines bright in the dim-lit room.

A tossed shoe, a leap, a dance,
Caught in folly, lost in chance.
Who knew fumbles made such a sound?
In this madness, joy is found.

A flash of color, a wild hair,
We strut and sway, without a care.
With noses crinkled and brows askew,
Our shenanigans continue to brew.

Laughter echoes as we dare,
In our chaotic, zany affair.
For in the dark, we're legends, you see,
Masters of glee, wild and free.

Glimmers of Grunge

Underneath that tattered lace,
Lies a smile, a wink, a trace.
With old records spinning round,
We dip and dive without a sound.

Mismatched socks and wild hair,
Twisted tales we often share.
Grunge so chic, it's all the rage,
As we dance and skip the stage.

A small mishap, a playful slide,
With every blunder, we take pride.
In this mess, we find our groove,
Glimmers sparkle, hearts they move.

So come along, ignore the trend,
Let's laugh loudly, let the fun extend.
In our universe, chaos will reign,
Glimmers of grunge, we'll entertain.

Veiled Vigor

Behind curtains of playful tease,
We gather strength like the buzzing bees.
With every laugh and every cheer,
Veiled vigor draws us near.

A quirky song on a clumsy beat,
We bounce along, bouncing on our feet.
Each silly dance a secret treat,
In shadowy corners, all's discreet.

Our antics mask, enchant, and dazzle,
Lost in moments that softly frazzle.
In this nook, we find our way,
Veiled in joy, come what may.

Whispers of fun in the darkened space,
With every twist, we embrace grace.
For vigor reveals its clever guise,
In laughter's glow, our spirit flies.

Fragments of Fire

In the twilight, sparks arise,
Fragments of fun caught in our eyes.
Each little giggle, a flame alight,
We dance in rhythms, pure delight.

Whirling like leaves, we take the stage,
With quirky tales on every page.
Our moments flicker, wild and bright,
In this whirlpool of sheer delight.

The world may fumble, but we won't cease,
Gathering joy like a light-hearted breeze.
Fragments of fire, we glow and gleam,
Woven together, we share the dream.

So come ignite this playful spark,
Join our revels in the dark.
For in our midst, the flames aspire,
A tapestry woven of fragments of fire.

The Irresistible Charm of Dusk

In the twilight glow, oh what a sight,
Laughter echoes, spirits take flight.
Bubbles of giggles in the dying light,
As mischief twirls, ready for the night.

Whispers of color dance in the air,
Cheeky grins bloom without a care.
Piggybacks, cartwheels, all in the flair,
Who knew dusk could be so unfair?

Jokes passed around like candy delight,
Witty retorts that spark in the night.
With each fleeting moment, a new invite,
To magic made just out of sight.

Glances exchanged, a laugh maybe shared,
Dusk holds secrets no one has dared.
With every step, a story prepared,
Irresistible charm so expertly bared.

Prowling Glamour After Dark

Strutting with flair under the moon's gaze,
Stars winking back in mischievous ways.
Heels click and clack on these vibrant lanes,
Where glamour meets laughter, all night it reigns.

Cloaked in allure, with a wink and a cheer,
Each shadow loves to whisper, 'Hi dear!'
The world is a stage, with schtick and a leer,
In this night of jest, it's all crystal clear.

Tempting the night with jokes that enchant,
Even the critters seem keen to prance.
Sassy banter leaves no room for grant,
In the theater of charm, we're all in a dance.

With glittering eyes, our mischief unfolds,
Tales wrapped in laughter, each one more bold.
Prowling with panache, as the night scolds,
Under the spell where magic beholds.

Caresses of Contempt and Grace

A roll of the eyes, a flick of the hair,
With a touch of disdain, but we don't really care.
Sassy remarks cut through the air,
Each jab we deliver is wrapped in flair.

With elegance poised like a waltzing star,
We dance through the night, both near and far.
Poking fun at the flaws, that's just who we are,
Grace in our chaos, a love-tattered scar.

Our humor's a edge, sharp as can be,
Yet kindness entwines with each playful spree.
In this lively bounce, we feel so free,
Cherishing each quip, raising spirits like tea.

Oh, the warmth of our laughter, caresses of glee,
In this game we play, there's no one but we.
With contempt so sweet, how great it can be,
A sassy parade, just let it all be.

Sassy Rhythms in the Gloom

In pockets of darkness, the beat does arise,
Whispers of laughter, like stars in the skies.
Movement and groove, oh what a surprise,
Sassy rhythms dance, as the world simply sighs.

A cheeky little chuckle, a wink from the shade,
Each step forward, new jokes trade.
In this carnival of light and charade,
The night's playful energy never will fade.

Grooving through chaos, sweet moments we chase,
A hop, skip, and jump, each one we embrace.
With swagger and laughter, we quicken the pace,
Transforming the gloom into our happiest place.

Lively and spirited, we own the night show,
In sassy attire, with pizzazz and glow.
Unruly and raucous, oh what a tableau,
With rhythm and humor, we steal the whole show.

Sizzle Beneath the Surface

In a world where giggles blend,
Witty banter is the trend.
Beneath the sparkle, mischief brews,
Ticklish tales in vibrant hues.

With glances sharp and smirks so sly,
We dance like bubbles in the sky.
A wink, a laugh, the charm ignites,
Creating chaos, sparking delights.

In corners where the bold reside,
Adventure waits, a playful ride.
With every twist, a jest unfolds,
Laughter's warmth, a tale retold.

So grab your friends, let's raise some cheer,
For silliness is always near.
With every chuckle, life's a blast,
Embrace the fun, forget the past.

The Charm of Cheekiness

A grin that dances on the lip,
With every prank, we start to trip.
Cheeky twinklings in our eyes,
Spreading giggles, sweet surprise.

We tease the frown, flip it around,
Beneath the jest, joy will abound.
With playful jibes and crafty schemes,
We turn the mundane into dreams.

Our laughter echoes through the air,
A sprinkle of joy, a cheeky flare.
A wink here, a nudge over there,
In moments stolen, we all share.

So raise your glass to good old fun,
In cheeky realms where pranks weigh a ton.
Let's sizzle through this playful spree,
The charm of mischief sets us free.

Lurkers of Liveliness

In every nook, the winkers creep,
With giggles low, they stir from sleep.
Lurking where the fun awaits,
Their laughter echoes, sealing fates.

Watch out for swipes and funny jests,
They pop up when you need the best.
With vibrant tales and banter bright,
They turn the mundane into delight.

With a twinkling eye, they pluck the strings,
Creating chaos, oh the joy it brings!
In playful paths where trouble dwells,
The lurkers spin their cheeky spells.

So join the dance, unleash your glee,
For liveliness beckons, can't you see?
With every chuckle, we'll take a chance,
To twirl in this playful, riffing dance.

Echoes of Enigma

Whispers bounce with a teasing flair,
In every puzzle, laughter's there.
With hidden pranks and sly disguises,
The enigma's charm never lies.

A riddle wrapped in mystery,
Each giggle holds a history.
Beneath the surface lies the tease,
Unlock the fun with playful ease.

In cryptic smiles and knowing winks,
We ponder meanings, quick as blinks.
Mirthful echoes paint the scene,
A tapestry of laughs unseen.

So step into the game with zest,
For every riddle is a quest.
With laughter's key, unlock delight,
Embrace the mystery, shine so bright.

Tints of Trepidation

In the corner, a giggle hides,
A playful sneer, where mischief bides.
Faint whispers won't dare reveal,
What antics roll with a squeaky wheel.

As shadows stretch beneath the sun,
Caution lingers but still we run.
Fun in every little scare,
With quirky friends, we banish care.

A blushing blush on cheeks aglow,
Every clumsy step, a funny show.
In laughter's clutch, we all take part,
With giggles darting, we brave the heart.

Underneath the jesters' grin,
Lies a joy that's bold within.
With tints of fear and hints of cheer,
We live for moments that draw us near.

The Gait of Grit

With every step, a wobble found,
A little stumble on the ground.
Sassy struts and an air of might,
Marching chaos into the night.

Watch the wobblers flaunt their pride,
Toppling dreams, they never hide.
With silly jiggles and bouncy flair,
No mockery here, just pure love to share.

Feet in rhythm, what a sight!
Unruly moves in pure delight.
The gait of grit, a sight to see,
In the dance of life, oh so free.

Watch out world, here they come,
With laughing snaps and joyful drums.
Each misstep sparks another cheer,
In this surreal parade, we all persevere.

The Snicker in the Dark

In the dusk where giggles creep,
A secret chuckle, a promise to keep.
Muffled laughter, a whispered jest,
In shadows, we find our quirky best.

Tales of blunders, the night's delight,
Echo in corners, a pure delight.
Creeping around with a playful fright,
We poke the gloom with eyes of light.

A sudden snort, a stifled grin,
The silly games begin to spin.
Shenanigans dance in the inky space,
In the grin of the moon, we find our place.

Through the dark, we scurry near,
With mischievous cheer and reckless cheer.
The snicker stirs, a feisty spark,
In this silly realm, we leave our mark.

Charisma in the Corners

Where corners lurk with charm and glee,
A quirky vibe speaks joyfully.
In the nooks where laughter swells,
The charisma here beguiles and tells.

Whispers spin from playful lips,
As the heartbeat of fun gently skips.
Sassy winks and laughter bright,
We twirl through corners, hearts alight.

With every glance, a cheeky view,
A playful world we gleefully pursue.
In crowded corners, wild and vast,
The charisma flows, a joyful blast.

Embrace the antics, let spirits soar,
With humorous flashes, we crave for more.
In little corners where giggles twine,
We paint the world with humor divine.

Defiant Silhouettes at Twilight

In twilight's playful glow, they dance,
With giddy steps, they take a chance.
Mischievous whispers cling to the night,
Creating curves in the fading light.

Sassy figures abound, bold and spry,
Chasing each other beneath the sky.
Laughter echoes, oh what a sight,
As they pirouette with sheer delight.

With antics that flaunt, they prance and tease,
Tripping on laughter, doing as they please.
Each silhouette rebels in its own way,
Defying the dusk, come what may.

As the stars twinkle, they spin around,
Defiant souls in merriment found.
In shadows, they weave tales of delight,
Creating mischief as day turns night.

Flirtations with the Night

When the moon winks like a playful friend,
The night is young, with time to spend.
Eyes glimmering bright, oh what a tease,
Whispers of laughter drift in the breeze.

With a twirl of skirts and a flash of grins,
They flirt with the dark where the mischief begins.
Each secret shared is a giggle on cue,
As they dance beneath stars, just a few.

In a game of chase, they dart and prance,
Embracing the oddities in their dance.
With every step, they nudge the moonlight,
Turning the night into pure delight.

Flirtations arise with a cheeky breeze,
Every glance shared, a spark to seize.
In the glow of the dark, they come alive,
Sassy spirits, unabashedly thrive.

The Sassy Tapestry of Secrets

Upon the loom of night, threads intertwine,
Crafting tales of mischief, oh so divine.
Each whispered secret a flourish bold,
In the tapestry of laughter, stories unfold.

Sassy stitches, vibrant and bright,
Woven with giggles, a marvelous sight.
Every knot whispers a daring plan,
As they spin round, a hilarious clan.

With a flick of the wrist and a grand display,
They stitch the fabric of night's cabaret.
A patchwork of grins in evening attire,
Creating a saga that never will tire.

In each playful thread, a story resides,
Wrapped in humor, where nothing hides.
The darkness can't dampen the fun they weave,
In the sassy tapestry, they believe.

Underneath the Bold Moon

Underneath a moon that holds its breath,
They frolic with joy, defying death.
With a giggly grin and a wink of the eye,
Each step tells a joke, flying high.

With boldly spun tales that tickle the night,
They dance in the moonbeams, feeling so right.
Every slide and shimmy ignites the air,
As laughter erupts, without a care.

The moon chuckles softly above their tread,
As they tumble and spin, lightly led.
In this raucous revelry, life feels so fast,
Creating memories that forever last.

With shadows as partners, they twirl in glee,
Celebrating the silliness, wild and free.
Underneath the moon, where joy takes flight,
They blossom and thrive, a charming sight.

Glimmers of Grit and Grace

In the alley where the cats play,
A dancer twirls in a bright ballet.
With mismatched shoes and curly hair,
She sidesteps pigeons without a care.

Laughter echoes through the street,
As ice cream falls, a tasty treat.
Her twinkling eyes, a comic sight,
Beneath the glow of the neon light.

Bouncing back from each small fail,
She wears her pride like a vibrant sail.
With each flub, she takes a stance,
A jester's heart in a daring dance.

Life spills joy in slanted rays,
Her quirky charm ignites the days.
Through giggles loud and antics grand,
She crafts a world that's truly planned.

The Charm of Untamed Spirits

In a tavern filled with hearty cheer,
A jolt of antics, the drinkers leer.
With winks and quips, she steals the show,
Her laughter sprouting like spring's first glow.

She weaves tall tales with playful flair,
Of dragons, treasure, and comets rare.
Each jest a spell, each wink a charm,
With tales that twist and then disarm.

Toast to the wild and the witty rogue,
With lime green drinks and a cat in a brogue.
When she takes the floor, all pause and grin,
Her dance spins tales of where we've been.

From barstool thrones, they hoot and cheer,
As legends rise with each fermented beer.
In laughter's grip, the night's embrace,
Turns mundane life into a funny chase.

Luscious Laughter in the Abyss

At the edge of night, where giggles gleam,
A pirate ship sails on a sugary dream.
With gummy worms and candy gold,
Their vivid tales of treasure unfold.

A parrot squawks in a rainbow hat,
Trading puns with a friendly cat.
With each hearty laugh, they digress,
Creating joy from whimsy's mess.

Into the void, their humor flies,
Through starry skies and sweetened pies.
Where gloom meets wit, it all collides,
And chuckles sprout like playful tides.

In the depths, where light breaks in,
Their laughter soon becomes a win.
So fear not the dark, for here we thrive,
With every giggle, we feel alive!

Dusk's Dazzling Detour

As twilight spills on the sidewalk's grace,
A troupe of mischief finds their place.
With juggling fruits and circus dreams,
They twinkle like stars in playful schemes.

Witty banter and cartwheels wide,
Each moment bursts with joy inside.
They dance along the cobblestone,
Painting the night in colors unknown.

With hiccups loud and slips so neat,
Their laughter pierces the evening heat.
As shadows mingle with giggling light,
Daring duos steal the night so bright.

Hand in hand, down paths unseen,
Through antics wild, their hearts convene.
In every flub, a tale is spun,
As dusk embraces their droll, free run.

Echoes of Insolence

In a world of chatter, loud and bright,
Little quirks take bold flight.
With a wink, a sass, a playful tease,
They dance around like buzzing bees.

Giggles echo in every crack,
Turning frowns, never looking back.
Poking fun at the serious pride,
With a grin so wide, they'll never hide.

Each step a mischief, a riotous game,
Flipping boring rules, not feeling shame.
In this vibrant charade, they thrive,
Bringing laughter, keeping joy alive.

So join the cavalcade, come take a turn,
For the art of cheek is what we'll learn.
Embrace the jests, let laughter sway,
In this raucous ballet, we'll frolic and play.

Silhouettes of Spice

In a realm where bold flavors clash,
Hearts ignite in a playful flash.
With a sprinkle of cheek and dash of zest,
They stir the pot and laugh with the rest.

Colors swirl in a comedic mix,
The secret's out, who needs to fix?
A pinch of sass and a dash of grin,
It's a buffet of fun, let the tasting begin.

Chasing the mundane out of sight,
Twisting and twirling, oh what a sight!
Each bite a giggle, a jovial tease,
In this flavorful world, we aim to please.

Come savor the joy, the sass and cheer,
With a hearty laugh, there's nothing to fear.
In these silhouettes, spice runs amok,
With every giggle, we'll never be stuck.

Reflections of Rebellion

In the mirror of life, they strike a pose,
Breaking the norm wherever it goes.
With a giggle here and a wink over there,
They challenge the chaos with flair and care.

Marching to rhythms that no one knows,
Flicking convention with playful throes.
In this carnival of quirky delight,
Rebellion never felt so light!

Jokes fly high, like kites in the air,
Why follow the crowd when you can dare?
With each little stunt, laughter ignites,
In this rebel crew, joy takes flight.

So raise a cheer for the playful knights,
With giggles and grace, they reach new heights.
In reflections of whimsy, the rules are bent,
Where laughter's the message, and the sass is sent.

Flickers of Flair

In the spotlight's glow, antics unfold,
With a bounce, a jig, and stories bold.
Each flicker a spark, a laugh in disguise,
Witty banter reflects in their eyes.

Like fireflies dancing on a warm night,
Chasing the mundane with bursts of delight.
A twirl, a twist, a fervent play,
In every move, they light the way.

Poking fun at the ordinary grind,
With each jest, a treasure you'll find.
In this theater of mirth, we embrace,
Every flicker, a jubilant trace.

So step right up to the comedy fair,
With laughter in pockets and light as air.
In flickers of joy, let your spirit dance,
With a quirk and a giggle, take your chance.

Hues of Defiance

In a world of colors bold,
Where laughter breaks the mold,
We paint the town with hues so bright,
Dancing in the strange twilight.

With every shade, a tale is spun,
Riddles wrapped in golden fun,
Brushes flick and swirl with glee,
Defying norms as wild and free.

Cerulean skies and fuchsia ground,
Echo giggles all around,
We strut with pride, mischief in hand,
Crafting chaos, just as we planned.

Oh, the palette roars its cheer,
Colors clash, but never fear,
For in this playful, vibrant mess,
We find our truth, our own finesse.

Glistening Grit

In the alley where the bravest play,
Sparkles dance, come what may,
Sweaty brows but smiles so grand,
We wade through life's golden sand.

Unfazed by mud, we strut and grin,
Glistening grit, let the fun begin,
With every stumble, laughter blooms,
Echoing through the funhouse rooms.

A cocktail mix of grit and glee,
Frolicking like it's meant to be,
Slip and slide, come take a chance,
Join the riot, join the dance.

Each scrape tells a joke so fine,
Shining bright, we freely shine,
In this comedy of errors bold,
Our tales of grit are spun in gold.

Tints of Tenacity

When life gets tough, we take a stand,
With colors bright, we stir the sand,
A crafty wink, a clever twist,
Grit and humor in every mist.

Emerald dreams and magenta foes,
With shades colliding, laughter grows,
We poke the bear, bring on the fun,
In a vibrant battle, we've just begun.

In quirky hats and mismatched shoes,
We strut with flair and nothing to lose,
Tenacity weaves through every line,
A canvas of brilliance, truly divine.

So let us paint with joyful might,
Creating wonders in day and night,
For in this jest, we find our way,
With tints of tenacity leading the play.

The Dance of Daring

In the spotlight, we twist and twirl,
With daring moves that make heads swirl,
A giggle here, a skip or two,
In this wild dance, we break through.

Step by step, we own the floor,
With every leap, we crave for more,
No rules apply when fun's the aim,
In this game of life, we stake our claim.

Stilettos high and hearts in flight,
We boogie down into the night,
With laughter ringing in the air,
Daring dreams beyond compare.

So come along and take my hand,
In this dance, a whimsical band,
Together we'll spin, jump, and sway,
Creating smiles, come what may.

Flares of Defiance in the Night

With a wink and a nod, they strut,
Bright colors bouncing, no ifs or buts.
They dance like fireflies, quick and spry,
Spilling laughter beneath the sky.

Their antics ignite a spark that's bold,
In every jest, a story told.
With each twirl, the night becomes bright,
A joyful riot, what a sight!

Jokes fly as they weave through the breeze,
Tickling minds with effortless ease.
Like stars that flicker and tease the eye,
They lift spirits, soaring high.

Embracing the chaos, they embrace the fun,
Playing till the morning, they've just begun.
With flares of defiance, they light the way,
In the heart of the night, forever they'll play.

The Sway of Irreverent Starlight

Glimmers of mischief, oh what a view,
As they sway like the leaves, absurd but true.
With each wild twirl, they challenge the norm,
In a universe where chaos can form.

Boundless giggles, like melodies float,
Echoing laughter, on whimsy they dote.
Upside-down smiles chase the moon's cheek,
In awe of the playful, so bold and so sleek.

From comets of giggles to pulses of cheer,
They slip through the night without any fear.
With stardust and whimsy, they celebrate grace,
In the sway of the night, they find their own space.

Each moment a gem, a twinkle divine,
As the universe winks, its humor entwined.
With a chuckle, they leap into the sky,
Painting the heavens with joy that won't die.

Eclipsed Snickers and Smirks

In a world where giggles eclipse the night,
Snickers are shadows caught in the light.
With every smirk, a plot they weave,
In the game of laughter, who would believe?

Whispers of fun dance on the breeze,
As friends join in, all eager to tease.
Under the cover of a mischievous grin,
They pull pranks that make the world spin.

Caught in a moment of shared delight,
Their humor ignites, an infectious sight.
Fleeting as fireflies, they flicker and play,
Chasing away gloom, come what may.

In the laughter's embrace, they twine and share,
With a wink and a laugh, forget every care.
In a universe filled with shimmers and quirks,
They revel in joy, eclipsed snickers and smirks.

Velvet Notes of Attitude

Wrapped in velvet, their attitude sings,
Stylish and sassy, they dance on the strings.
Every step a story, with flair and with grace,
A tapestry woven, in a jubilant space.

Their laughter is music, sweet and jazzy,
Shaking up norms, they make things hazy.
With a flick of the wrist and a glance oh-so-bold,
They shimmer like fabric, vibrant and gold.

Chasing the night with a teasing delight,
In swirls of charisma, they dazzle the light.
A wink here, a grin there, they know how to charm,
In the fabric of fun, they keep us all warm.

Riding the waves of their velvet-toned tunes,
They redefine rhythm beneath playful moons.
With each note they hit, the world feels alive,
In their playful pursuit, we all learn to thrive.

Unapologetic Whimsy

With a wink and a grin, they prance around,
Clad in colors that never quite brown.
Jokes in their pockets, mischief on cue,
Even the sun laughs at the things they do.

They twirl like confetti, so bright in the air,
Living each moment without a care.
Chasing their giggles, they tumble and fall,
Life is a carnival, they answer the call.

Their laughter a melody, sweet as can be,
Bobbing like bubbles in a sprawling sea.
Watch them dance wild, a joyful parade,
In a world that's daft, they're the grand charade.

So here's to the whimsy, bold and carefree,
Life's a big joke, come join the spree!
No need for the serious, or stares that are sour,
Just pure, unfiltered, whimsical power.

Silver Linings in a Sassy Twilight

In twilight's embrace, the stars start to wink,
With sass that could make the clouds stop and think.
Glittering dreams float on whispers so sweet,
Dancing on rooftops with nimble little feet.

A cheeky moon grins as he wobbles his light,
Casting a glow that feels oh-so-right.
Giggling at shadows that stretch on the street,
The night has a rhythm, a playful heartbeat.

Fizzy pop laughter fills the cool evening air,
With every wisecrack, a twinkle to share.
Chasing stars with plans that don't need a map,
Life's a cheeky adventure, a whimsical lap.

So raise up your glass to the twilight so bright,
Where silver linings wink with pure delight.
In this cheeky dance where joy takes the lead,
Every moment's a treasure, a reckless creed!

Where Spice Meets the Dark

In the corner of dusk, where flavors collide,
Bottles of laughter and mischief reside.
With a dash of delight, they stir up the fun,
Waltzing with shadows as day meets the sun.

A sprinkle of chaos, a pinch of surprise,
The echoes of giggles light up the skies.
Sassy concoctions in a bubbling brew,
Crafting a potion of wildness anew.

So grab a spoonful of sugar and cheer,
As they sauce up the night with raucous good cheer.
Lively and daring, they dance on the brink,
Spicing the dark with the colors they think.

Cackles and chuckles, the recipe's right,
Turn down the mundane, pour joy into the night.
Where spice leads the way, and shadows play tag,
Life's a saucy affair, let's raise up the rag!

Mischief in the Evening Glow

As daylight surrenders, the mischief awakes,
With giggles and grins, the sly laughter shakes.
Beneath orange skies where the cool breezes blow,
The antics unfold in a charming tableau.

With night just a swish, they plot and they scheme,
Catching starlight in a whimsical dream.
Bouncing on laughter like marshmallows whirl,
Every twinkle a wink in this cheeky pearl.

From rooftops to gardens, the pranksters shall roam,
Chasing the twilight, where fun feels like home.
Jaws drop at the capers, mirth fills the air,
In the glow of rebellion, no moment to spare.

So here's to the mischief, unbridled and bright,
In the cozy embrace of the softening light.
With giggles and glares, let the antics grow,
For mischievous hearts steal the evening glow!

Sparks of the Spunky

A squirrel in a hat makes its move,
With acorns in tow, oh, what a groove!
It dances on branches, twirls with flair,
Who knew nuts could lead to such a dare?

The pigeons all stare, their beaks in a cluck,
As the cheeky little critter runs amok.
With twinkling eyes, it chases a bee,
Laughing aloud, 'Come and dance with me!'

A leaf on the ground, a stage for two,
An audience gathered—a whole birdview!
With flips and with flops, they steal the scene,
Life's better in jest—know what I mean?

So, tip your hat to the spunky and bright,
For laughter and antics make everything right.
In moments of silliness, joy will ignite,
And life's quirks will shine, oh what a sight!

Vignettes of Vivacity

In a café, a cat wears a bow,
Pausing mid-yawn, putting on a show.
The barista spills coffee; it splashes with glee,
'Oh darling,' it purrs, 'No harm done to me!'

A dog with a donut trots down the street,
Dodging the pigeons, what a treat!
He prances with joy, tongue flapping about,
Life's sprinkled with sugar, of that there's no doubt.

A turtle in shades keeps up the chase,
While rabbits gather for a slow-paced race.
They're giggling and strutting, the stops in between,
Life's a wild party, a whimsical scene!

So here's to the moments that jostle our soul,
With laughter and mischief, we dance to the goal.
In every small vignette, let joy be the key,
For fun is the heart of true vivacity!

Flashes of a Flare

A flamingo in sneakers struts by a pier,
Winking at fish with an elegant cheer.
With a swish and a spin, it calls out, 'Hey friends!',
'Life's a big party; let's dance till it ends!'

A gecko on rollerblades zooms down a wall,
Its tiny helmet secure, it's having a ball.
It flips like a pro, such a sight to behold,
With laughter and thrill, the magic unfolds.

In the park, there's a squirrel with a cape,
Rescuing acorns, it's hoping to escape.
With a leap and a twirl, it stops for a pose,
Life's full of surprises, as everyone knows!

So keep your spirits high, let silliness flare,
Join in on the fun, there's plenty to share.
With giggles and grins, let's brighten the air,
For laughter's the spark that ignites everywhere!

Flames of Finesse

A llama in shades sipping tea on a mound,
Exclaims, 'I'm the trendiest beast to be found!'
With a flick of its tail and a wink of its eye,
It struts like a star, oh my, oh my!

A parrot with style boasts tales oh so grand,
Of jungles and pirates and treasures so planned.
With a squawk and a flap, it dazzles the crew,
In this circus of life, it commands the view!

A penguin in bowties slides down the ice,
With wobbly grace, oh, isn't it nice?
It dances in circles, a dab here and there,
Just a fun little guy with a flair for the rare!

So toast to the silliness, let laughter suffice,
For laughter and joy are truly our spice.
In moments like these, let our spirits caress,
Embracing each bump with flames of finesse!

Surges of Sassy Spirit

Lips are painted, bright and bold,
With every wink, a story told.
Strutting feet, they tap and spin,
Each swirl declares, "I'm here to win!"

Laughter drips from every glance,
In this chaos, we twirl and prance.
With flicks of hair and heightened heels,
We chase the fun; it's what we feel.

Giggles bubble at every turn,
In playful tricks, our spirits burn.
We're a riot of color, flair,
Crafting mischief in the air.

So if you see us, don't be shy,
Join the party, come on, fly!
With sassy spirits, we ignite,
A vibrant world, shining bright!

Embers of Enticement

Chasing glances, hearts ablaze,
With teasing smiles, we set the phase.
Dancing lightly on the edge,
Of cheeky jokes and dainty pledge.

In swirling skirts, we twirl around,
With every laugh, a spark is found.
A finger beckons, come on near,
In this quick wit, we find our cheer.

Like fireflies in the summer night,
We shimmer, twinkle, everything bright.
Our giggles launch like firework bursts,
In the game of charm, we quench our thirst.

Enticing tales, we weave so grand,
With playful jabs, a flirtatious band.
So let you join this merry dance,
With us, dear friend, take a chance!

Shadows in Heels

Heels click-clack like a beat on repeat,
Every step, we conquer the street.
With laughs that echo and smiles that twinkle,
We're the stars that forever sprinkle.

In playful jests, we mock the night,
Turning whispers into sheer delight.
With every strut, we lead the scene,
Elevated queens, we reign supreme.

Glances exchanged, like winks in the dark,
We draw them in, igniting the spark.
With our bravado, we break the norm,
In this wild ride, we're the storm.

Unearthly giggles, a mischievous song,
For in these heels, we feel so strong.
Join us now, let's dance and play,
In this grand tale, we'll find our way!

A Wink at the Wild

In the moonlight's glow, we come alive,
With cheeky grins, our spirits thrive.
Our laughter vibrates, a rhythmic call,
Enticing the daring to join our thrall.

With tousled hair and playful flair,
We dance through life without a care.
A wink here, a nudge there,
In this delightful game we share.

Pouncing on fun like it's our feast,
We weave wild tales, never the least.
In this adventure, we are free,
Champions of joy, come dance with me!

With mischief brewing, hearts afire,
We spark the wild, lifting each desire.
Join our crowd, let's break the mold,
In this spirited dance, be brave and bold!

Edges of Entropy

In a world of quirk, we tiptoe bright,
With mismatched socks, oh what a sight!
The cat's wearing shades, strutting so cool,
While we dance around like silly fools.

Paper plans drift, like leaves in a breeze,
Laughing at chaos, if you please.
Coffee spills, and vows gone astray,
Yet we wear our mess like it's our play.

We twirl with flair, break every trend,
Each laugh a sparkle, a joyful blend.
In the corners, our giggles collide,
Embracing the chaos, let hearts abide.

For in this whirl, life's a comedy,
Where quirks gather, setting us free!
With a wink and a grin, we take the stage,
In this fun-filled folly, we share our age.

The Aura of Attitude

With a smirk and a toss of our hair,
We walk the line, a daring pair.
In mismatched shoes, we strut with pride,
Creating a scene, oh what a ride!

Lipstick smiles and cheeky bars,
We own the night, like rockstar stars.
Glances exchanged, sparks in the air,
Confidence glowing, without a care.

In a world of norms, we draw our maps,
Tickling chaos with our little mishaps.
Laughs echo loud, a delightful tune,
As we sway to the beat of our own cartoon.

With swagger unmatched, we twirl and spin,
Finding the magic beneath our skin.
Each pose a frame, a timeless dance,
In our little world, we take a chance.

Glare of Glam

In a dazzle of sparkles, we shimmer bright,
With glitter in hair, we daze the night.
Sipping on laughter, with flair we glide,
In a world of whimsy, we take pride.

Strutting on air, like peacocks gone mad,
Our antics contagious, we make life rad.
With sunglasses on, we own the scene,
In this wild adventure, we reign supreme.

Dresses that twirl with a mind of their own,
We make our mark, like seeds we've sown.
Loud cheers and winks, in colors so bold,
Our tales of glamour are a sight to behold.

As moonlight glimmers, we laugh and cheer,
In this circus of life, we persevere.
With a twinkle in eye and a step so grand,
We dance through the night, hand in hand.

Sassy Serenade

In a tune of giggles, our voices rise,
With silly rhymes and playful lies.
The world can wait, we're on a spree,
With our catchy jingle, join in with glee!

We sing of pies that fall with a splat,
Of cats in pjs and a dancing hat.
Every step a melody, we chuckle loud,
In this carefree dance, we feel so proud.

Every note a spark of radiant fun,
Under the sun, our shenanigans run.
Our sassy song floats up into space,
With quirks and charm, we embrace our grace.

So grab your friends, let laughter lead,
A sassy serenade, plant the seed.
With every chorus, we claim our trail,
In this joyous rhythm, we shall prevail!

Playful Darkness Unleashed

In the corner lurks a sneaky grin,
Whispers of trouble, let the fun begin!
Dancing with mischief, a cheeky delight,
Twinkling eyes sparkle in the night.

Chasing the giggles, we scatter like mice,
Each little faux pas a roll of the dice.
In the twilight, we're jesters unbound,
With every misstep, we leap off the ground.

Oh, the antics we pull, like cats on a spree,
Wearing our chaos, wild and free!
In this playful ballet, we all take a part,
With a wink and a laugh, we dance from the heart.

With quirky demands and puns that don't cease,
We're giggling so hard, we've lost all our peace.
In our frolicsome world, who needs a plan?
While trouble is brewing, we're the best, yes, we can!

The Radiance of Rebellion

With paint on our cheeks and hair out of place,
We strut through the night with a daring grace.
Rebelling with laughter, we're breaking the norm,
Creating a ruckus, a perfect storm.

In a world of suits, we wear colorful threads,
Twirling like whirlwinds, unbothered by dread.
Our shoes may be mismatched, but we don't care,
In the spotlight of chaos, we flourish and flare.

We laugh in the face of those who conform,
We dance in the rain, embracing the storm.
With giggles like fireworks lighting the sky,
We savor each moment, let our spirits fly.

Outcasts with flair, we're the kings and the queens,
Living our lives in ridiculous scenes.
So join us, dear friend, in this carnival ride,
Where humor and madness and brilliance collide!

Glistening Moments of Boldness

With bubbles and giggles, we toast to the night,
In moments of boldness, everything feels right.
We spin fresh ideas like a whimsical wheel,
Laughing at gravity, can't hold back the feel.

From dainty confetti to crowns made of cheese,
Crafting our mischief with utmost ease.
We jump into puddles, splash colors anew,
With every bold step, we write something true.

Twinkling in laughter, we sparkle and shine,
Each mischievous act is a sip of divine.
Our boldness a beacon, guiding the way,
In a world painted vibrant, let us dance and sway.

So gather, dear friends, let's toast to the flair,
To those glistening moments we all can share.
For laughter's the gem we always pursue,
In the bright of the night, we'll paint it anew!

Specters of Chic Audacity

In the realm of the daring, we parade with style,
Draped in audacity, we stroll for a while.
With a wink and a nudge, we charm every glance,
Specters of sass in a whimsical dance.

We tiptoe on rooftops, in heels made of light,
Our laughter echoes through the soft, starry night.
Witty one-liners weave through the air,
Every outrageous outfit a bold, brazen dare.

With cheeky banter, we rattle the calm,
Mixing laughter and chic like a sweet herbal balm.
The night wears our courage like glimmering gold,
In moments of fun, so audacious and bold.

So here's to the misfits, the ones who stand tall,
With humor as armor, we conquer it all.
In a world painted bright with audacious finesse,
With style and with laughter, we tailor our mess!

The Riff of Resilience

With a wink and a grin, we rise again,
Laughter's our armor, through thick and thin.
Jokes round the corner, like socks in the wash,
Finding the funny, turning a posh nosh.

The Edge of Elegance

Twirling in heels, with humor so grand,
We dance through the chaos, a quirky band.
Dresses of sparkles, a mess of delight,
Tiptoe on giggles, all day, all night.

A Cackle in the Shadows

Hiding behind laughter, we lurk and we play,
Chasing the giggles that dance in the fray.
Whispers of jesters, the world turns to jest,
In a land of chuckles, we're simply the best.

The Lure of the Lively

With a bounce in our step, we're never too tame,
Life's a wild party, the punchline's the game.
Jovial journeys, with mischief in sight,
Join in the fun, we'll laugh till we're bright.

Pulse of the Unseen

In the corner, it whispers, a giggle so sly,
It dances on edges, where bold spirits fly.
A wink in the dim light, a cheeky little tease,
And suddenly, silence is shattered with ease.

The clock ticks with mischief, each beat finds a prank,
While laughter erupts from the depths of the dank.
In coats of the night, all the quirks come alive,
With antics so silly, watch the gigglers thrive.

Subtlety struts with an outrageous flair,
As humor blooms brightly, painting joy in the air.
You can't stop the playful, it wiggles and spins,
In a world full of nudges, we wonder who wins.

So raise up your glass to the unseen delight,
To jests that keep blooming, both day and by night.
A whirl of the whimsical, let laughter ensue,
For all of the chuckles, oh yes, that's our cue!

Silvery Sass

Beneath the full moon, they skitter and sway,
With glimmering giggles that lead us astray.
A twirl and a tap, what's that underfoot?
Oh dear, just the mischief that gave me the boot!

In fanciful frocks, they parade all around,
With hair made of starlight, they leap off the ground.
A wink of their eyes sets the world all aglow,
As sass flares with laughter, oh don't you just know?

They prance through the sparkles with bows on their heads,
And tickle the fancies while dancing in beds.
Each shimmer a tease, each giggle a prize,
In the realm of the cheeky, oh, how time flies!

So let's join the frolic, let merriment last,
With quirky companions, we'll revel and blast.
For life is much brighter with a wink and a grin,
With silvery sass, let the good times begin!

The Glint of Gumption

With a hop and a skip, the daring ones roam,
In glittering garb, they make mischief their home.
Each chuckle a spark, each leap is a tease,
Their laughter erupts like a wild summer breeze.

Like fireflies flickering, they zip through the night,
Creating a ruckus, those jesters of light.
With gumption aplenty, they chase down the fun,
And outwit the snoozers, 'til dawn's early run.

They twirl in the moonbeams, so sassy and bold,
With stories of wonders that never get old.
The glint in their eyes reflects joy on display,
They spin all the troubles, and toss them away!

So here's a salute to the merry brigade,
With a wink and a jest, let's party unafraid.
For gumption's the heartbeat that makes spirits sing,
In this whimsy-filled world, joy is the king!

Shades of Sass

A flicker, a flash, what's that in the air?
It's mischief on tiptoes, concealed everywhere.
With curves full of charm, they waltz through the trees,
In the glow of the twilight, they dance with such ease.

Their antics are bright, like confetti in flight,
With jokes tucked away, just waiting for night.
Each nudge and each wink, a prank to behold,
The cut-ups alight, with stories retold!

From whispers to giggles, they flutter about,
Creating a ruckus, they're never in doubt.
With sass in their steps, they flip every frown,
Transforming the gray skies to a vibrant town!

So let's raise a cheer for the playful brigade,
The shades of those jesters, in glee we paraded.
In the revelry's warmth, let our spirits be free,
For laughter's the magic, and joyous decree!

Whispers of the Audacious

Beneath the moon's cheeky grin,
Laughter dances, soft and thin.
Echoes of mischief prance about,
In giggles wrapped, without a doubt.

Sassy breezes tease the trees,
Tickling leaves with playful ease.
Footsteps tap in quirky styles,
Chasing giggles, chasing smiles.

With winks and grins, they take their stand,
A merry band across the land.
Each jest a sprinkle, light as air,
Tickling those who venture there.

So let us frolic, let us sway,
In this humorous ballet.
For in this realm where jokes abound,
The laughter leaps, the joys resound!

Daring Echoes in Dusk

When twilight giggles, echoes laugh,
Adventures plot a comical path.
With jests that twirl like glittering stars,
They unearth fun from near and far.

A zesty wind, a brazen tease,
Whispers daring, such a breeze.
Chortles pop like fireflies bright,
In the fading glow of playful light.

Beneath the sky, we spin and weave,
With every quip, we dare to believe.
Like jesters bold, we strut and play,
Turning mundane into a cabaret.

Freed from worries, we toss and roll,
In this frolicsome, jolly stroll.
Echoes of daring will wane with night,
Yet in our hearts, they spark delight!

Veils of Vivid Attitude

Under the glow of streetlamp's cheer,
Character struts, drawing near.
With attitude wrapped in a funky wrap,
Friends gather close for a whimsical clap.

Expressions bold, in colors bright,
Fashioned antics take their flight.
Each chuckle a thread in the fabric spun,
A tapestry woven, laughter begun.

Daring glances, cheeky grins,
Sparking joy where mischief begins.
Each twist and twirl, a playful charm,
Safety found in this raucous arm.

So wear your attitude, bright and proud,
Join the lively, merry crowd.
In vibrant veils, we find our peace,
Hearts a-twirl, our joys release!

The Playful Dance of Dusk

As dusk descends with a wink and sway,
It beckons laughter to come and play.
In a playful jig, the world ignites,
Dancing feet in shimmering lights.

With each twirl, a giggle spills,
Sprinkling joy atop the hills.
In corny jokes, we take our flight,
Improv moments painted bright.

So raise a glass to silly tunes,
As stars peek out, wearing croon.
The playful dance we all embrace,
In silly socks and a happy face.

Through dusk's embrace, we laugh and cheer,
In every chuckle, love draws near.
Let joy unroll like ribbons cast,
In this playful dance, we hold steadfast!

Attitude Adrift

I waltz with my quirks, so delightfully bold,
With sneakers on clouds, my story's retold.
Flip my hair like a flag, let the world take a guess,
In a sea of pink flamingos, I'm dressed in finesse.

With a wink and a grin, I cause quite the stir,
Bubbles of laughter, just watch them confer.
My sidekick's a cat with a penchant for flair,
Together we conquer, giving mischief a scare.

Sipping on sass, it's my secret elixir,
While others march on, I'm the dance floor's mixer.
Each step that I take, it's a laugh and a leap,
In a galaxy of giggles, where the oddballs creep.

A crown made of crumpets, a throne built of fun,
Dancing on tables, oh, isn't it one?
With each playful jest, my spirit takes flight,
In a world full of chaos, I'm the spark and delight.

The Allure of Audacity

Oh, to strut like a peacock, bright feathers in view,
Eating dessert first, yes, that's what I do!
I skip over seriousness, flip it on its head,
While others play nice, I'm the one who's well-fed.

With mischief in my pocket, I light up the room,
My tales spun like webs, inviting the zoom.
Why color inside lines when I can doodle outside?
In chuckles and giggles, I take so much pride.

I'm the jester in court, with a sly little grin,
Cracking jokes that leave folks wondering where they've been.
Spinning tales of lunacy, oh, what a delight,
Each word is a sparkle, each laugh is a flight.

When life hands me lemons, I dance in the rain,
I make lemonade cakes, then go back for more gain.
So here's to the brave, who color with flair,
In a world so outrageous, we'll never despair!

Radiance of Rebellion

I dance with the moon, with stars in my hair,
In the glow of the night, watch me strut without care.
My heart is a canvas, each beat paints the air,
In a riot of colors, you can't help but stare.

With laughter as fuel, I blaze like a jet,
Steering through life, oh, no sign of regret.
Is that a wild giggle? Oh yes, it's just me,
Unfolding my quirks in delightful spree.

Breaking out of routines like they're made of soft cheese,
With every bold step, I do as I please.
In the flares of my spirit, a joyful brigade,
In a world full of echoes, I'm the vibrant parade.

From sitcom scenarios to whimsical dreams,
I ride on the waves, fueled by laughter's sweet beams.
Wearing chaos like jewels, in a quirky array,
In the heart of rebellion, I frolic and play!

Colors of Confidence

With paint on my cheeks and joy in my veins,
I strut down the street, embracing my reigns.
Weaving through doubts like a pro-fancy dancer,
In the carnival of life, I'm the wildest prancer.

Each compliment's a canvas, I splash it with glee,
With a wink to the doubters, 'Just watch, you'll see!'
In a world of drab grays, I bloom like a flower,
Invoking giggles, I savor each hour.

My footsteps make music, each laugh a crescendo,
Dancing on rainbows that flow from my window.
With colors that shatter the silence of doubt,
I spark up the room, that's what life's all about.

So here's to the bold, let our pennies be spent,
In the market of laughter, where joy is the rent.
With shades all around, oh what a grand sight,
In a world full of color, I'm the burst of delight.

www.ingramcontent.com/pod-product-compliance
Lightning Source LLC
Chambersburg PA
CBHW071836160426
43209CB00003B/319